COMMUNITY · CONNECTIONS

?

WHAT DO THEY DO?
DOCTORS

BY JOSH GREGORY

CHERRY LAKE
Publishing

Published in the United States of America by Cherry Lake Publishing
Ann Arbor, Michigan
www.cherrylakepublishing.com

Content Adviser: Leonard Feldman, MD, Assistant Professor of Medicine and Pediatrics, Johns Hopkins School of Medicine
Reading Adviser: Cecilia Minden-Cupp, PhD, Literacy Consultant

Photo Credits: Cover and page 1, ©Andresr, used under license from Shutterstock, Inc.; page 5, ©Ronald Sumners, used under license from Shutterstock, Inc.; page 7, ©iStockphoto.com/jsmith; page 9, ©iStockphoto.com/iofoto; page 11, ©iStockphoto.com/sjlocke; page 13, ©iStockphoto.com/ImagineGolf; page 15, ©Erwin Wodicka, used under license from Shutterstock, Inc.; page 17, ©iStockphoto.com/stevecoleccs; page 19, ©iStockphoto.com/LionHector; page 21, ©forestpath, used under license from Shutterstock, Inc.

LIBRARY OF CONGRESS CATALOGING-IN-PUBLICATION DATA
Gregory, Josh.
  What do they do? Doctors / by Josh Gregory.
     p. cm.—(Community connections)
  Includes bibliographical references and index.
  ISBN-13: 978-1-60279-805-2 (lib. bdg.)
  ISBN-10: 1-60279-805-2 (lib. bdg.)
  1. Physicians—Juvenile literature. 2. Medicine—Juvenile literature.
I. Title. II. Title: Doctors.
  R690.G736 2010
  610.92—dc22   2009042801

Cherry Lake Publishing would like to acknowledge the work of The Partnership for 21st Century Skills. Please visit www.21stcenturyskills.org for more information.

Printed in the United States of America
Corporate Graphics Inc.
July 2010
CLFA07

DOCTORS

CONTENTS

WHAT DO THEY DO?

A TRIP TO THE DOCTOR

You wake up one morning to get ready for school. You don't feel so well, though. Your mom feels your forehead. She uses a **thermometer** to check your temperature. It is too high! It's time to visit your doctor.

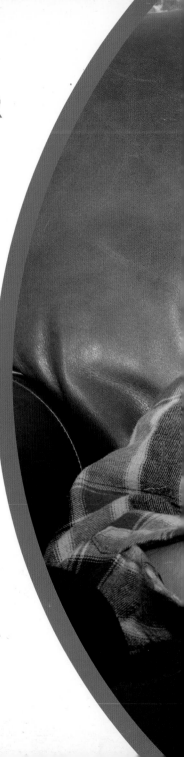

When you're not feeling well, you should see your doctor.

A doctor asks questions and listens carefully. He uses a **stethoscope** to hear your heartbeat and breathing. He looks down your throat and in your ears. He shines a light in your eyes. These tests help a doctor figure out what is wrong. He may give you **medicine**.

A doctor listens to your heartbeat and breathing.

Sometimes you see your doctor just for a checkup. She will talk to you about good health habits. She may give advice about what food you should eat. She may also talk to you about exercise and rest. The doctor will make sure you have all your **vaccines**.

A doctor can give you advice about staying healthy.

People go to school for many years to become doctors. Why do you think this is? Think about how many different sicknesses there are. Now think about the ways to treat them. A good doctor knows about almost all of them!

HOW DO DOCTORS HEAL US?

Doctors can do more than just give you medicine when you are sick. Have you ever gotten hurt while playing outside? Have you ever fallen off your bike? A doctor can treat cuts and bruises. He can also fix broken bones.

A doctor can fix a hurt wrist.

Doctors use **stitches** to help heal bad cuts. The stitches a doctor uses are a lot like the ones used to make your clothes! The doctor cleans out the cut really well. Then he uses a needle to stitch the cut shut. This helps the cut heal quickly. Without stitches, big cuts can take a long time to heal.

A doctor uses stitches to treat a big cut.

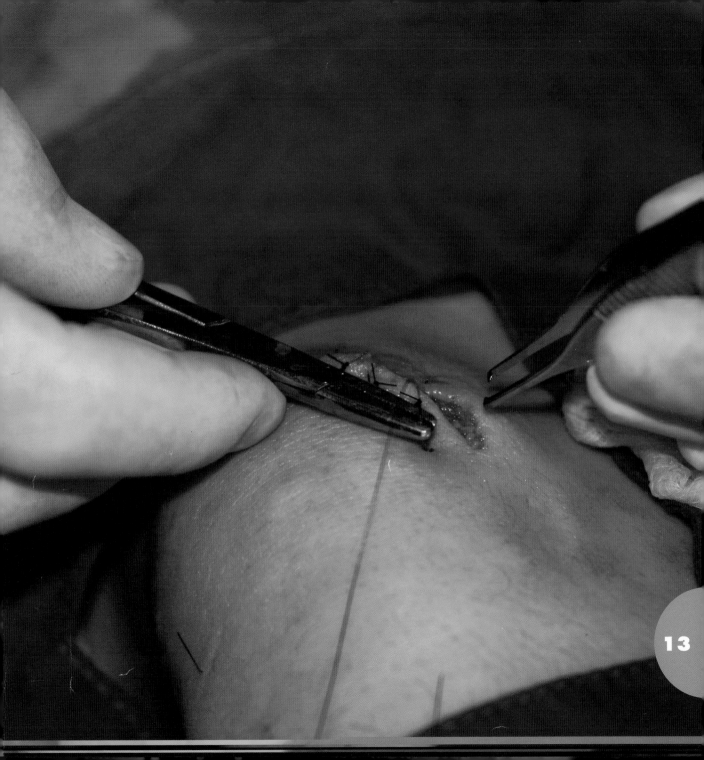

13

Doctors also have a special way to fix broken bones. First, they use an **X-ray** to look at the bone. Then they put the bone back in place. Next, they put on a hard covering called a cast. This keeps the broken bone from moving around as it heals.

A doctor will use a cast to help heal a broken bone.

Why do you think a broken bone needs a cast? Does it help protect the bone? How does it help the bone heal? Do you think a broken bone would be able to heal correctly without a cast?

15

DIFFERENT KINDS OF DOCTORS

Sometimes people are very sick. They go to doctors called **specialists**. These doctors go to school longer than other doctors do. They learn everything about one kind of illness or body part. This helps them become experts at treating those illnesses or body parts.

Some doctors are experts on people's brains.

Do you know anyone who has had an **operation**? Doctors called **surgeons** perform operations. Some work on peoples' brains. Others fix hearts.

Some doctors work only on one group of people. For example, they might treat only children. Others help people who have **allergies**.

Surgeons are doctors who perform operations.

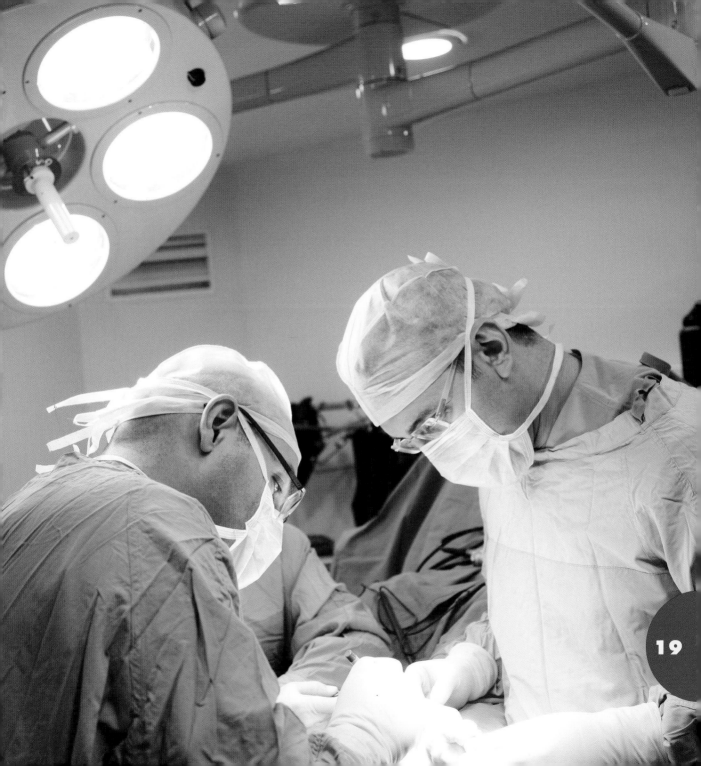

Doctors work long hours. Sometimes they even sleep at the hospital. People can get hurt or sick at any time. Doctors often rush to the hospital at night or on weekends.

We need doctors to keep us healthy. We should always remember to thank them for the important work they do!

Doctors work long hours to care for their patients.

Being a doctor is not an easy job. It takes a lot of time and hard work. Why do you think people choose to become doctors? Ask some doctors what reasons they had for picking such a hard job. You never know what you might find out!

GLOSSARY

allergies (AL-ur-jeez) reactions to substances such as pollen, foods, or drugs

medicine (MED-uh-suhn) a drug used to treat a sickness

operation (op-uh-RAY-shuhn) a procedure in which a person's body is cut open to repair damaged parts

specialists (SPESH-uh-listss) doctors with special training

stethoscope (STETH-uh-skope) an instrument doctors use to listen to patients' hearts and lungs

stitches (STI-chiz) loops of threads used to close a cut

surgeons (SUR-juhnz) doctors who perform operations

thermometer (thur-MOM-uh-tur) a device used to measure temperature

vaccines (vak-SEENZ) shots that help prevent diseases

X-ray (EKS-ray) a special picture that shows parts of the body that cannot be seen from the outside

FIND OUT MORE

BOOKS

Buckley, James Jr. *A Day with a Doctor*. Mankato, MN: The Child's World, 2008.

Heath, Erin. *Doctors in Our Community*. New York: PowerKids Press, 2010.

WEB SITES

KidsHealth—WORD! A Glossary of Medical Words
kidshealth.org/kid/word/
Look up easy-to-understand meanings of medical terms.

KidsWorld: Becoming a Doctor
www.kidzworld.com/article/9229-becoming-a-doctor
Learn all about what it is like to work as a doctor.

INDEX

ABOUT THE AUTHOR

Josh Gregory writes and edits books for children. He lives in Chicago, Illinois. He once wanted to be a doctor.